The Color of Longing

Haiku

by

Philip Kenney

Finishing Line Press
Georgetown, Kentucky

The Color of Longing

Haiku

Copyright © 2025 by Philip Kenney
ISBN 979-8-89990-236-9 First Edition
All rights reserved under International and Pan-American Copyright Conventions. No part of this book may be reproduced in any manner whatsoever without written permission from the publisher, except in the case of brief quotations embodied in critical articles and reviews.

Publisher: Leah Huete de Maines
Editor: Christen Kincaid
Cover Art: Alamy Stock Photos
Author Photo: Pitman Piyavatin
Cover Design: Elizabeth Maines McCleavy

Order online: www.finishinglinepress.com
also available on amazon.com

Author inquiries and mail orders:
Finishing Line Press
PO Box 1626
Georgetown, Kentucky 40324
USA

For Georgio

ACKNOWLEDGMENTS

Since no book is a solo act, I prefer to place acknowledgments at the beginning, not the end. I write haiku before I wake up in the morning. That's right, I often wake to seventeen syllables running through my mind. I write haiku in the shower, while trying to meditate, on my morning walks: just about everywhere. But I am lost as to judging which are fit to include in a book and where to place them. For that, I am deeply indebted to my wife, Lori, my son, Georgio and friend and poet John Brehm for helping these haiku find their special spot in this manuscript. My dear friends are an endless source of encouragement, support, good conversation and laughter. They are my pals. You know who you are. How do you thank the ineffable? Call it what you will, the muse, the creative spirit, the unconscious voice—the impulse and guidance to put words together has become my nearly constant companion I could no more live without than my family and friends. That relationship enlivens everything and extends to the world and its infinite variety of subjects. My thanks to all of the above and any I may have left out.

Preface

Haiku are swallows, dragonflies—changing directions in a flash. And when that happens, the world is illuminated. They surprise and delight and enable new ways of seeing, a shift in consciousness.

Haiku are childlike. They look at the ordinary facts of life—a bird on a branch, sunlight on water— and bring to life the extraordinary quality of the living.

It has been said that haiku are the expression of the poet's epiphany. As such, they are nectar for the poet and the reader, as captured by Basho's poem.

In short, with just a few simple words, haiku satisfy the longing in the human heart for beauty and connection. They bring us closer to the mysterious, yet palpable, sacredness of being that captures us in an instant.

May these haiku touch that longing in you.

With Gratitude

Even in Kyoto—
hearing the cuckoo's cry—
I long for Kyoto

Matsuo Basho
(1644 - 1694)

Translated by Robert Hass

our pond is the blue
  of alpine lakes
      the color of longing

ducks leave the pond
a few laugh
like drunken wind

			before sunrise
			   an oblong moon
			      slips down a chimney

I write while it's dark
with the curtain pulled down—
silence holds the pen

amber sunlight
on the lake—
I pause for a drink

     even among trees
          bathing in sunlight
               I long for trees

summer night
          Saturn and Venus
                    steal the show

my landfill is full
it won't hold one more regret,
yet I pile them on

out of emptiness
stillness
out of stillness—
everything!

    dragonfly
        you turn so fast—
            make up your mind!

    swallows circling
        august light betrays
            the poor little bugs

old woman
    pumping gas
where are your teeth?

dawn
over coastal hills
    sparkling surf

            wild pigeons in flight
    white wings flashing
                    through gray

                    she sings in the dark
                with other voices, longing
                    to become a song

    mother is a cloud
        billowing, slowly adrift . . .
            dissolving into blue

    circles of sunlight
    resting on Sequoia bark
        going nowhere

the day is young
　　outside my window
　　　　　　an owl hoots

　　　　she likes to be
　where the sky can find her
　　　　wind combed hair

a train whistle blows
waking the sun from its dream—
that familiar tune

he walks
to not hear himself
walking

I like the old guys
Basho and Issa, Buson
    it's the same old sky

I feel I have lived
forever—

am I wrong?

the bashful rosebud
　undresses in solitude
　　erotic dream

a western screech owl
　　sings to the darkening wild—
　　　　crickets keep the beat

I like nothing more,
than to gaze at the wild things
until I am gone

      swift little bush tits
    swarming the suet feeder
          leave for a nice bath

little blue pup tent
perched on a sidewalk's edge
      who sleeps inside you?

        last night of summer
     a chorus line of crickets
                     not ready to die

snow melting slowly
  the day has lost its luster,
     sleds no longer slide

            the plump towhee
         a narrow stem bends
              with its weight

      a purple halo
    circles the moon
        old men sigh

    two chubby racoons
        keep an eye on me
            one stands and glares

                I smooth the bedspread
              trying to remove wrinkles—
                      the cat is amused

there's a pond in the park
I discovered it today
sitting on a bench

in clear water
a galaxy
    of tiny bubbles

summer's last word
    thunders over the city
        this old house shakes

    one branch bows
one leans into the sun
              I walk beneath both

            cherry blossoms
              have not
                forgotten us

```
        early fog
resting on calm water—
        nothing moves
```

```
a nail in the wall
        where a photo
                        once
                hung
```

it's over now
the bell is still . . .

hear it?

snowflakes pause
born again as plum blossoms
        before the slow fall

        the fog has lifted—
it only takes a moment
            to make a poet

    dark skies won't budge
the full moon takes a night off—
      a comet's in town!

    the varied thrush
     does not vary
       its call

    Song Sparrow
blowing its trumpet—
   the sky weeps

        right about now
            I need a dog
                to lick my face

afternoon breeze—
    cherry blossoms
        settle on a squirrel

morning walk—
ten thousand simple things
to fall in love with

chestnut leaves
you startle me—
when did you open?

Basho's haiku
pebbles on still water
ripples far and wide

leaves are coming
    I'll miss the skeletons
  reaching for the sky

                  we never questioned
              the absence of questions—
                      I wonder why?

a flash of haiku—
    the night sky
            trembles

breakfast on the porch
mornings of such loveliness
I forget to eat

first rose
of the first bloom—
clocks melt

Children of the Streets:

someone's little girl
asleep on a concrete bed,
her knees tucked up

someone's little boy
bare ass, shouting at devils
        someone's little boy . . .

    a mother's child
staggering, falling
through a jungle of despair

Beethoven in the kitchen
making breakfast
with our son

                    rainfall
            pools of immense
                  happiness

an empty pillbox
medicine finds its mark—
swallowed days

don't worry
words will never desert you
yearning draws them in

The Coastal Redwoods

   amongst giants
    overcome
       by quiet

   the cathedral is open—
      we walk softly
           over the body of years

   charred and jagged trunk—
     the lightning strike
       was precise

          the sound
      of ten thousand leaves
          clapping

slowly new buds
   emerge from the stem
        quickly they fade

       two lives
          at the feeder
       feeding

   that face
          gray as fog—
             death hovers

    trees sway leisurely
their leaves whisper
        I am swept away

               dreaming
           on a faultline
                of shame

green has never been
so green, nor blue so blue—
dragonflies circle

the earth turns
light becomes shadow—
my many moods

I wonder,
does the old bent oak
feel young too?

      those who sit
    and look become
         the quiet pond

About the Author

In early 2023 **Philip Kenney**'s first book of haiku, *Only This Step*, was published by Finishing Line Press. Poet John Brehm said of this work, "These poems pay homage to the great haiku masters and bring a fresh energy and perspective to the form." Prior to writing haiku, Mr. Kenney published The *Writer's Crucible: Meditations on Emotion, Being and Creativity*, which was a finalist for the 2018 *Red City Review* Non-Fiction Book of the Year. He is also the author of the novel *The Mercy Dialogues* and a collection of essays entitled *So Many Surprises*. Mr. Kenney writes and practices psychotherapy in Portland, Oregon.

www.ingramcontent.com/pod-product-compliance
Lightning Source LLC
Chambersburg PA
CBHW030100170426
43197CB00010B/1600